Report by the South West
Economic Planning Council

Retirement to the South West

London   Her Majesty's Stationery Office

914·235
ENV

91674

Published for the Department of the Environment

0129498

ISBN 0 11 750999 X

Members of the South West Economic Planning Council

Chairman

J L Thomas, BA; Senior Lecturer and Staff Tutor in Economics and Industrial Studies, University of Bristol

Vice-Chairman

Captain The Rt. Hon. The Lord Digby, DL, JP; Vice-Lieutenant of Dorset; Member, Dorset County Council

Members

Councillor B H Bailey, JP; District Organisation Officer, National and Local Government Officers Association; Member, Somerset County Council; Chairman, South Western Regional Health Authority

V H Beynon, BSc; Senior Lecturer in Agricultural Economics, University of Exeter

J L Bulley, MA(Cantab), MBIM, LTI; Divisional Director, John Heathcoat & Co Ltd

D K Clarke, CBE, MA; Economic Consultant

N R F Collins, FRTPI, SP Dip, ARIBA, Hons Dip Arch, MIT Dip; County Planning Officer, Gloucestershire County Council; Chairman, South West Regional Sports Council

D M Gillespie; Director, Olivers (Barnstaple) Ltd

Councillor W Graves, JP; Member, Bristol City Council; Member, Avon County Council

Councillor M W Green; Member, Dorset County Council

D J F Hunt, MBE, LLB; Solicitor

Mrs K E Lambert, JP, BSc(Econ), FRHS; Chairman, Southern Gas Consumer Council

W G Mitchell; Bristol Branch Secretary, Society of Lithographic Artists, Designers, Engravers and Process Workers

R S Pascoe; South West District Delegate, Amalgamated Society of Boilermakers, Shipwrights, Blacksmiths & Structural Workers

N J L Pearce, LLM; Director of Administration and County Solicitor, Avon County Council

P Pensabene, CEng, FIEE, MInstPI; Chairman, Philip Group, Dartmouth

J H Perry; Managing Director, P & H Hotels (Torquay) Ltd

Councillor D E Phillips; Member, Cornwall County Council

N J Record; Company Planning Manager, C & J Clark Ltd

Councillor P M Robins; Solicitor; Member, Gloucestershire County Council; Chairman, Gloucester City Council

A L Sayers; Member, Devon County Council

The Rt. Hon. The Earl of Shelburne; Member, Wiltshire County Council; Chairman, North Wiltshire District Council

D A Smith, CEng, FIMechE, FIProdE, JP; Managing Director, Hamworthy Engineering Ltd

P Sutcliffe; Chairman, Devon Community Council; Chairman, Dartington Hall Ltd

W E Vince; South West District Organiser, Furniture, Timber and Allied Trades Union

Councillor G G Walker, JP; Chairman, Avon County Council

S J West; Local Director, Barclays Bank Ltd, Exeter District
Mrs P Woods; Member, Devon Conservation Forum; Farmer
G C Wyndham, DL, BA, JP; Member, Somerset County Council

Secretary

Mrs A M Humphreys; Department of the Environment, Froomsgate House, Rupert Street, Bristol BS1 2QN

Contents

Contents

Foreword

For a long time now people have been leaving other parts of the country to live in the South West on their retirement. This is the direct consequence of the region's attractive environment and climate. The migration has been increasing over recent decades and its concentration into the more popular areas has prompted some public debate.

The consequences to a community which arise from having a high proportion of retired people are both many and complex. Whilst some may cause difficulties, others provide advantages. Communities of predominantly elderly people present social problems both for the elderly themselves as well as for the rest of the communities. The demands on public services in the health and welfare field may be increased to an extent not offset by reductions in demand for other services, such as education. There are fears that the migration of retired people will add to the pressures in some favoured seaside areas which are already approaching the physical limits for residential development. The movement into the region of people making new homes on retirement brings gains in local spending power and this prosperity of individuals will in turn affect the demand on public services. Indeed, such prosperity can raise property values (and rateable values) to the detriment of the local working population. In assessing the situation, the contributions of retired people to social activities and the voluntary services of a community must not be overlooked.

Looking at this complex problem, the South West Economic Planning Council therefore decided that they should seek to find a clearer picture of the role which retired people play in the economic life of the region. This report is a summary of the study, which was undertaken at the Council's request by Mr I R Gordon of the University of Kent. The report excludes Mr Gordon's detailed methodology (which can be obtained from the address below at a cost of £1·00) and presents his statistical findings and inferences as simply and directly as possible.

There are no statistics of the actual numbers who, on retirement, have moved to the South West. Migration is anyway a two-way process : there are many people who move out of the region on retirement, whilst others who move into the region on retirement move away again when a husband or wife dies. However, the number of retired people in the region is known and the report identifies statistically the number of retired people additional to what one would have expected had the region conformed to the national average pattern. They are described in the report, for convenience, as the 'additional retireds'.

The study shows that the retirement issue, as thus defined, figures much less in the total regional picture than has been commonly supposed. It is estimated that there were about 138,000 'additional retireds' in 1971, out of a regional population of just under 4 million. If present trends continue, the number might grow to about 155,000 by the end of the century. This is a considerably slower growth than that of the whole regional population. The study also confirms that retirement plays a positive part in the regional economy. The incomes of the 'additional retireds' account for perhaps 5 per cent of total personal income in the South West, while their expenditure adds some £54 millions annually to the income for local communities ; this last figure compares with the estimated £115 millions annually for the income-generating capacity of the region's holiday industry. Perhaps some 44,000 or so jobs are dependent on the presence of the 'additional retireds'.

Mr Gordon's study did not cover the other side of the coin – the cost to the regional economy. The Council found that no information was readily available which could be analysed to determine the costs of providing public services for the 'additional retireds'. However, health services are substantially funded from the Exchequer and the Rate Support Grant formula takes account of the number of persons over retirement age in each local authority area. Looking at the problem regionally, therefore, the available Central Government support towards the needs of the 'additional retireds' should reach the region. The balance of the costs has to be met locally and whether the contribution of the 'additional retireds' equates with these costs is not known. However, the Council are satisfied that, with the small scale of retirement migration, a further regional study of the economic aspects is not justified.

The Council recognise the limitations of the material in the report. We have also necessarily had to exclude from consideration the social implications of retirement which are also highly relevant in the popular locations. Nevertheless, in presenting this analysis of the economic aspects our aim is to contribute to the deeper understanding of the retirement problem which is vital for future planning in the retirement areas of the South West.

The Council are grateful to Mr Gordon for the work he has undertaken in a field which has not attracted from economists the attention which it merits.

South West Economic Planning Council
Froomsgate House
Rupert Street
Bristol
BS1 2QN

July 1975

1 Introduction

1.1 Nationally, retirement does not generate a positive economic role. Indeed, some of the most obvious characteristics of the retired are that they are economically inactive, have standards of living which on average are well below those of the working population, and make net demands on the economic resources of the nation, particularly on the public sector. In many areas of the South West Region, however, the immigration of retired people plays a positive role in local economies. The capital and non-employment incomes which the retired bring to the region provide the basis for considerable expenditure on locally-produced goods and services. In fact, in these areas the retired may be thought of as all-the-year-round holidaymakers, providing an external source of local demand similar in kind, and possibly not far behind in scale, to that of the holiday industry.

1.2 Immigration of retired people is not of course confined to the South West. It exists also in other coastal areas of the country, including much of the South Coast, parts of Wales, and the Fylde in the North West. But in these other regions it is important only locally – along a coastal strip or in individual spa towns – or at most sub-regionally. In the South West, however, largely because of the region's peninsular situation, the effect is geographically much more widespread. Virtually all the south and west of the region is involved, as well as more localised areas in the north.

1.3 This report is primarily directed to the economic effects of retirement migration to the South West. The aim has been to highlight aspects which are of relevance to strategic planning in the region. This concentration of attention means that many other important economic and social issues affecting the retired or the elderly population in general have been excluded from consideration.

1.4 These other issues do of course have implications for the region. Changes in the financial position of the elderly, in the range and scale of social services for their support, in the types of accommodation built for them, in national policy towards retirement age, would all have important consequences for the South West. Retirement migration itself raises important social questions, in terms, for example, of its desirability from the point of view of the migrants themselves and of the most suitable forms of community provision for the elderly. These more qualitative questions are also outside the scope of the report, which is concerned only with the desirability – the economic costs and benefits – of retirement migration seen from the viewpoint of the host region or communities. This concentration of attention inevitably means that many other important social and economic issues affecting the position of the retired or elderly population in general have been ignored.

1.5 A further parallel between retirement migration and the holiday industry is that each is concerned with a better enjoyment of leisure time obtained in consequence of movement from one area to another – usually a once-for-all movement of course in the case of the retired migrant. The origins of both are thus similar. The modern holiday industry emerged initially from a background of travel undertaken mostly for religious, educational or medical purposes (witness the success of the spas in the late 17th Century). But its roots, particularly in the South West, lie mainly in the last century with the development of the seaside resorts offering a change of environment within the means of a very much wider range of people. The earliest large-scale retirement migration to the South West was also mainly directed to the provincial cities and spas, but by the middle of the 19th Century it had become a feature of the coastal resorts. Common factors have influenced the growth of both retirement migration and holiday making – for instance, greater mobility for the individual with the coming first of the railways and then of the motor car, and the opportunities for better leisure enjoyment associated with increasing national wealth and rising real incomes and pension and holiday provision. Increasing urbanisation and the high cost of accommodation in more densely populated parts of the country have probably also been important factors in the movement to the South West.

1.6 Retirement migration makes greater demands on land than the holiday industry. In the more popular retirement areas of the region the operation of planning policies restricting the supply of land for housing results in increased house prices and thus acts as a method of rationing. The result has been some geographical spreading of retirement activity, although on a restricted scale so far, possibly because of the strong pull of the mild climate of the older resorts along the southern coast of the region and because the retired are less immediately mobile than motorised holidaymakers.

1.7 The progress of retirement migration in the South West has also lagged behind the regional holiday industry. There are several explanations. Perhaps the most fundamental is that social inequalities have tended to be much more marked among those over retirement age than among the working population. Another important factor is that retirement migration is mainly confined to people who own their own homes. The considerable growth of owner-occupation among the younger working age groups during the last 20 years has yet to make its full mark on the rate of retirement to the region. Retirement migration has been spreading down through the income groups during this century, and by the 1960s a significant number of former manual workers had started to appear among the migrants to the region's retirement areas. The continuation of these trends would mean the development of a larger and less exclusive population of retirement immigrants in the future. Indeed, if this process continued unchecked, this group would become, in due course, a much larger sector than the region's holiday industry, at least in terms of requirements for land.

1.8 Future planning for retirement migration must rest on a deeper understanding than there is now of such matters as its economic impact and the motivations of migrants. This report is intended as a first step in this direction, with the principal aim of establishing, quantitatively where possible, the broad outlines of this factor in the region — its scope, size, structure and rate of growth. The findings are based on existing sources of data, principally the censuses of population; no special survey was made of retired migrants.

2 The retired population of the region

Numbers

2.1 In 1971 about a quarter of a million men and half a million women living in the South West were older than the statutory pension ages of 65 for men and 60 for women. They represented 19% of the total regional population compared with 16% nationally. Not all those over retirement age were actually retired however, while, conversely, the region's retirement community would include some people in younger age groups. Including wives and widows of retired men, it is estimated that actually-retired people in the region totalled about 600,000 in 1971, or 16% of the regional population compared with 13% nationally. Almost two-thirds of these retired people were women and about 8% of the men were under the statutory pension age.

2.2 The absolute size of the retirement community in any area is of course of significance, particularly for the planning of public services on which the elderly make heavy demands. But retirement as such is not unique to the South West, and this report is primarily concerned with those who migrate to the region on retirement. They can be seen as comprising the 'additional' numbers of retired people in the South West — the number over and above that generated by the normal process of ageing of the region's resident population. As a convenient shorthand, this report refers to this element of the retirement community as the 'additional retireds', in contrast to the remainder of the retired population who are termed 'indigenous retired'.

2.3 From the point of view of analysis of the economic impact of retirement, the additional retireds group is particularly important for three main reasons. First, expenditure of this group represents a source of demand from outside the region for local products and services; second, the group represents that part of the retirement community whose geographical distribution might most reasonably hope to be influenced by regional and local planning policies; third, as the report notes later, the characteristics of retirement migrants probably differ in important respects from the resident retired group.

2.4 It is not easy to measure the numbers of the additional retireds as thus defined, and various estimating methods are open. A comparison with the national population structure suggests that the additional retireds account for nearly a quarter of the retirement community of the region. In relative terms, the additional retireds are more important in the South West than in any other region, though the South East Region with its major retirement areas on the South Coast leads in terms of absolute numbers. (The data in this report was compiled before Local Government re-organisation and the Bournemouth area is therefore included as part of the South East Region; this important retirement area is now within the South West Economic Planning Region.)

2.5 Table 1 indicates the broad sub-regional distribution of the additional retireds. As can be seen from the chart at Appendix 1, they form a significant part of the total population only in the Exeter-Torbay sub-region.

2.6 Table 1 also brings out that the additional retireds, like the holiday industry, are concentrated in the southern and western half of the region, with the Exeter-Torbay sub-region accommodating 40% of the regional total and the South East sub-region a further 20% or so. The only sub-region with an apparently significant shortfall in the numbers of retired is North Wiltshire, but this feature is exaggerated by the recent rapid growth in people of middle age following planned overspill to Swindon.

Table 1 : Geographical distribution of the additional retireds[1] : South West Region, 1971

| Sub-region | Additional retireds | | Total population ('000s) |
	Numbers ('000s)	Percentages of South West total	
North Gloucestershire	1	1	465
Bristol-Severnside	15	11	930
North Wiltshire	−7	−5	345
Wellington-Westbury	3	2	260
South East Area[2]	25	18	570
Exeter-Torbay	51	37	465
Plymouth Area	16	12	345
West Cornwall	17	12	265
Bodmin-Exmoor	17	12	215
South West Region[2]	138	100	3,850

[1]. For definition see text.
[2]. Excludes Bournemouth and Christchurch Districts.

Structure

Sex ratios

2.7 Women account for about two-thirds of the total regional population over retirement age. This male/female imbalance is, in small part, the consequence of the lower statutory retirement age for women and the higher mortality rate among men in the decade before retirement. Principally, however, it is the result of the greater life expectancy of women surviving to retirement age which is a national demographic characteristic.

2.8 The proportion of women among the region's actually retired population is slightly less, estimated at 64% in 1971. But the regional average disguises sub-regional variations, and the proportion of men seems to be larger in the major retirement areas, implying that the additional retireds include significantly more men than the indigenous retired population. This difference might merely be a reflection of the generally younger age composition of the additional retireds, but it could also reflect other factors, such as widows of the additional retireds returning to their original areas or differences in mortality rates between the additional retireds and others of the same age.

Age

2.9 The age structure of the retired population of the South West is somewhat younger on average than in other regions, as Table 2 indicates.

Table 2 : Estimated age structure of retired males, 1971

| Sub-division | Percentage of retired males | | |
	Under 65	65–70	Over 70
Northern	5·7	33·5	60·8
Central[1]	7·1	32·4	60·5
Southern	8·2	33·8	58·0
Western	8·1	33·1	58·8
South West[1]	7·1	33·3	59·6
Great Britain	5·8	34·6	59·6

[1]. Excludes Bournemouth and Christchurch Districts.
Source : 1971 Census of Population.

2.10 Since the difference between the regional and national picture is concentrated on the males under 65 it must be attributed mainly to premature retirement. The difference is most marked in the popular retirement areas. The implication is that the prematurely retired account for one-eighth or more of the region's additional retired males : many more would have been under 65 when ceasing to work and coming to the region.

Households
2.11 Clearly the housing requirements of the retired differ in important respects from those of the population at large. Qualitative information about the particular needs of the region's retired population is very limited but official statistics do indicate the size distribution of households with elderly members. In the South West, as in the country as a whole, about one-quarter of those over 65 lived in single person households in 1971 and a further half in two person households. The proportion living in a single person household was actually rather lower in the retirement areas of the region, possibly because they have fewer of the very old or widowed, and of young single people living in flats.

2.12 The proportion of the population over retirement age in the South West living in non-private households was quite small but a little higher than the national average (6% compared with 5%). Table 3 shows, however, the difference is wholly attributable to the numbers staying in hotels and boarding houses in the region ; the proportions in other sorts of institution were very similar to the national figures.

Table 3 : Proportions of the population over retirement age in non-private households, 1971

	South West Planning Region (%)	Great Britain (%)
Psychiatric hospitals	0·8	0·8
Other hospitals	1·6	1·6
Homes for the old and disabled	1·9	1·7
Hotels and boarding houses	1·4	0·5
Other non-private households	0·3	0·5
All non-private households	6·0	5·1

Source : 1971 Census of Population.

Social composition

2.13 Comparison of the social composition of retired men in Great Britain and the South West, on the basis of their former occupations, shows that the region has a rather greater concentration of the professional and managerial groups and a markedly smaller proportion of men from manual occupations. But this relatively small imbalance for the regional retirement community as a whole in comparison with the national picture becomes particularly marked for the additional retireds. The statistics suggest that the professional, managerial and technical groups account for about 40% of the male additional retireds in the South West, compared with only about 20% in the retired male population nationally. In contrast, the manual groups account for only a third of the region's retirement groups compared with over a half nationally. This bias towards non-manual groups is shared with other retirement areas and is partly a reflection of the stronger disposition of owner-occupiers to move away on retirement. But the social selectivity of the additional retireds in the South West in particular cannot be fully explained in these terms.

2.14 As with other characteristics of the additional retireds, their social composition varies significantly within the region, particularly between the Plymouth and West Cornwall sub-regions on the one hand and the other major retirement areas on the other. In the latter, including the Exeter-Torbay, South East Area and Bodmin-Exmoor sub-regions, there is a very marked imbalance between the professional and managerial groups and the manual groups and the socio-economic composition of the additional retireds in these areas seems very similar to that of the retirement areas of South East England. In contrast, the Plymouth and West Cornwall sub-regions appear to have smaller proportions of former non-manual workers, with a majority of their additional retireds drawn from manual occupations.

Rate of growth

2.15 Table 4 shows the changes which have taken place in the last half century in the numbers of people in the region over retirement age.

Table 4: Population over retirement age: South West Region and Great Britain, 1921-71

	South West Region[1]		Southern and Western Sub-divisions[2]		Northern and Central Sub-divisions[1]		Great Britain
	Numbers ('000s)	Percentages	Numbers ('000s)	Percentages	Numbers ('000s)	Percentages	Percentages
1921	289·9	10·5	115·9	11·0	174·0	10·2	7·8
1931	355·1	12·4	140·8	13·1	214·3	12·0	9·6
1951	519·2	15·7	201·1	17·2	318·2	14·9	13·5
1961	600·8	17·1	233·7	19·6	367·1	15·9	14·7
1966	652·1	17·8	255·2	20·8	396·9	16·3	15·4
1971	741·7	19·3	291·4	22·5	450·3	17·5	16·3

[1]. Excludes Bournemouth and Christchurch Districts.
[2]. Estimated for earlier years from Devon and Cornwall figures.
Source: Population Censuses.

2.16 Between 1921 and 1971 this element of the regional population rose from 290,000 to 740,000 people, a slightly slower rate of growth than nationally. The growth has been fairly constant, at about 2% per annum, though it seems to have accelerated somewhat in the latter 1960s after a spell of rather slower growth between 1951 and 1966.

2.17 This picture of steady growth in total numbers disguises the important changes which have taken place in the sources of growth. Up to 1951, the increase in numbers over retirement age was essentially a reflection of the process of natural change. The continuing steady rise in the 1950s and 1960s was, however, the consequence of large-scale migration of the elderly from other parts of the country to the South West. In the last two decades therefore, and particularly between 1966 and 1971, the proportion of the regional population in these age groups has increased consistently faster than nationally.

2.18 This relatively fast migration-led growth of the elderly population over the last 20 years has of course taken place alongside a comparable growth in the pre-retirement age population. For about a 100 years previously, the South West's share of the national population had declined persistently, reaching its lowest recorded level at the 1931 Census. But since 1951, most age groups and most areas of the region have experienced rather faster population growth rates than in other parts of the country, though in the Southern and Western sub-divisions the acceleration of growth in the retirement age groups preceded that in the younger population by about 10 years. In fact it was not until the latter 1960s that the pre-retirement age population of these two sub-divisions showed signs of growing faster than nationally.

2.19 These various trends are reflected in the changing proportion of the population over retirement age. As Table 4 shows, the regional trend has been consistently upwards, but there have been differences between the eastern and western halves. The former, the Northern and Central sub-divisions, still has an above-national average proportion in these age groups, but there has been a fairly steady movement towards the national average. In the Southern and Western sub-divisions, however, the proportion of elderly people has increased consistently faster than nationally during the past 50 years. In the earlier part of the period this trend mainly reflected the outward movement of younger people from these parts of the region; more recently, it reflects inward retirement migration.

2.20 Changes in the numbers of the additional retireds are less easily calculated, but estimates based on the available data suggest that they accounted for very similar proportions of the total regional retirement age population in 1951, 1961 and 1971, showing that the origin of large-scale retirement migration to the South West pre-dates 1951. Numbers of the additional retireds are estimated to have risen by 56,000 between 1951 and 1971, an increase of over 50%. However, here again there have been sharp differences between the eastern and western halves of the region. Over the 20-year period, the number of such retireds in Devon and Cornwall (roughly the Southern and Western sub-divisions) appears to have more than doubled, while those in the rest of the region have increased by only about a quarter. Thus, the general trend seems to have been for retirement migration to be directed progressively westwards, as the more accessible coastal areas filled up or became more expensive, with Cornwall emerging as a major growth area in this respect in the last decade. Indeed, with a 5% annual growth in numbers of the additional retireds in Devon and Cornwall over the last 20 years and with this growth representing a quarter of the total population growth in the two counties between 1961 and 1971, this must have been one of the fastest growing sectors of the economy of the far South West.

2.21 Analysis of trends in the Council's 20 Economic Planning Areas provides a more detailed picture of the distribution of the increase in the region's elderly population during the 1960s. The rate of growth in numbers over retirement age did not vary very significantly between the different Economic Planning Areas. Nevertheless, percentage rates of growth alone, often representing only small numerical changes, are not a helpful guide to the sub-regional changes that have taken place; it is better to look at the absolute growth in relation to the total population of an area. On this criterion, two of the Economic Planning Areas, South East Devon centred on Torbay and South East Dorset centred on Poole, emerge clearly as the most important growth areas for retirement to the region. In each, the increase in numbers over retirement age between 1961 and 1971 amounted to about 7% of their 1961 populations and accounted for nearly 60% and 30% respectively of the population growth in the two areas. (Appendix 2 shows that larger percentage contributions to population growth are found in the Forest of Dean, South West Dorset and North Cornwall, while without the increase in the population over retirement age there would have been a decline in the population of the Cotswolds and Exmoor). In the case of South East Devon, this trend was essentially a reinforcement of its long-standing role as the principal retirement area of the South West. The substantial growth in South East Dorset, however, appears to reflect a significant increase in the attractions of the area for retirement migrants. Most of the other areas in the southern and western parts of the region experienced roughly similar rates of growth, around 5% of the 1961 populations. The exceptions were the Salisbury, Plymouth and North Cornwall Economic Planning Areas where the rates of increase in relation to total 1961 population were substantially lower and comparable to those in the northern part of the region.

2.22 Estimates of the additional retireds element in the increase in the regional population over retirement age highlights four main areas of absolute increase in numbers of additional retireds – the South East Dorset, Exeter-East Devon, South East Devon and West Cornwall Economic Planning Areas. These four areas seem to have shared more or less equally in the growth in the numbers of additional retireds in the region during the 1960s. The estimates also indicate that it is the West Cornwall Economic Planning Area that has grown most in status as a retirement area in the last decade. At the other end of the region, the size of the retirement migrants group in the Bristol-Severnside Economic Planning Area seems to have cut back sharply during the period. This probably results from the substantial economic growth in the Bristol area. The additional retireds in this sub-region were based essentially on Bath (and to a lesser extent Weston-super-

Mare), rather than Bristol, but physical constraints had come to restrict any further growth in Bath. At the same time, Bristol's growing size seems to have encouraged an outward movement of retirement migrants. Taking the whole of the northern part of the region together, however, the recorded gains and losses over the period appear to cancel out, suggesting that much of the migration may have been over comparatively short distances.

Patterns of migration

2.23 From the evidence available, it would seem that retirement areas are amongst the most attractive for migrants in all age groups except the youngest working age group, for whom economic factors are a more important influence on where they want to go. For example, in 1961-1966 the net migration into the South West of people of retirement age was 25,000; for the two working age groups of 25 to 44 years and 45 to retirement age it was 27,000 apiece; but for the youngest age group, 15 to 24 years, it was only 7,000. In contrast, net migration into the South East Region in the same period was 46,000 for the 15-24 years working age groups with a net outward flow for all other age groups. The Census data also brings out clearly that the locational preferences among the youngest working age group have great importance for regional growth, since the mobility rate of this group is higher than for any other age group, and is three times higher than the mobility rate among people over 45 years old.

2.24 Migration between regions is not of course a one-directional movement, and even in the retirement age groups there are large flows in both directions. For instance, the net migrational gain to the South West between 1961 and 1966 of 25,000 people of retirement age was the balance between 44,000 inward moves and 19,000 outward moves. The number of outward migrants was in fact comparable with the numbers for the more industrialised regions such as the West Midlands, the North West and Yorkshire and Humberside, all of which had substantial net losses of retirement age migrants. There is some evidence that the outward migrants were more likely to be female and rather older than the inward migrants, but the outward movement is clearly not solely the result of return migration by bereaved widows. The greater part of it should perhaps be regarded as evidence of migration 'failures', possibly reflecting a lack of adequate prior information about the implications of retirement from a home area to a coastal retirement area.

2.25 For retirement age migrants to the South West, at least, an indication of the relative 'unattractiveness' of the migrants' home areas can be obtained by considering the ratios of inward and outward movements between the region and other parts of the country. The most significant movements in favour of the South West came from the conurbations, particularly the West Midlands conurbation and Greater London. This comparison highlights the apparent preference of the retirement migrant for less heavily urbanised environments.

2.26 Estimates made of the changes in the age and sex structure of net migration to the South West during the 1961-1971 decade reveal high levels of net migration into the principal retirement areas of persons in the 5 year age group immediately preceding the statutory retirement age. Indeed, the peak age for migration for retirement to the region seems to be about 62 for men and about 60 for women.

2.27 Comparisons of the two periods 1961-1966 and 1966-1971 indicate that the direction of net regional migration in the older age group changed during the decade. In the Northern sub-division, a net migrational gain between 1961 and 1966 in most of the age groups over 45 years seems to have been succeeded by net migrational losses between 1966 and 1971. In the Southern sub-division, no significant difference between the two periods can be discerned. In the Central sub-division however, and more strongly still in the Western sub-division, the trend of net migration in both the older working age and the retirement age groups appears to have been clearly upward.

2.28 The size of the additional retireds element in the regional population which would ultimately be generated by a particular rate of net migration among the over-45s can be estimated from the survival rates for each age group. Table 5 below sets out estimates for this ultimate size.

Table 5: Projected increase in the additional retireds: South West Region

Sub-region	Projected number of additional retireds ('000s) assuming constant migration at:	
	1961-71 rate	1966-71 rate
North Gloucestershire	2	−13
Bristol-Severnside	6	−2
North Wiltshire	1	1
Wellington-Westbury	6	−2
South East Area[1]	47	64
Exeter-Torbay	62	62
Plymouth Area	1	3
West Cornwall	15	9
Bodmin-Exmoor	19	32
South West Region[1]	159	154

[1]. Excludes Bournemouth and Christchurch Districts.

2.29 Comparison of the projections in Table 5 with the estimates in Table 1 earlier in the report indicates that the present numbers of additional retireds in the region as a whole would not increase very greatly if migration continues at the level of recent years. In some parts, notably Bristol-Severnside and the Plymouth Area, the numbers would probably fall. In the South East Area, however, and possibly in Bodmin-Exmoor, the projection of recent trends implies a very substantial increase in the additional retireds.

2.30 Nevertheless, these projections of future numbers can be no more than tentative, since there can be no certainty that the future rate of net migration will not be faster or slower than in the recent past. There are factors which imply that the rate will carry on increasing somewhat as it has done since the mid-1950s; these factors include the growth in home ownership between successive generations of the retired, the wider experience of holiday-making in the region and the pressure on housing in the more urbanised areas from which most retirement migrants come. On the other hand, there could be other influences at work which depress the rate of net migration, for example, smaller numbers of elderly people in the national population or the fact that some of the most popular and older-established retirement areas in the region may be approaching residential saturation.

3 Economic aspects

3.1 This chapter moves on from consideration of the characteristics of the retired population to an assessment of their impact on the regional economy, making use of a number of new estimates of income and expenditure associated with the retired. Few of the figures are based on direct measurement but they should be sufficiently reliable to indicate the more important economic consequences of retirement migration for the region.

Incomes of the retired

3.2 There is no information about the incomes of retired people as such, but the Department of Employment's annual Family Expenditure Surveys provide a source from which estimates can be made. It would seem that the retired are on average one of the poorest groups in the country, with average household incomes in 1971 less than 40% of the level in households with heads younger than 65. Household incomes have some relevance as an indicator of the financial well-being of the retired since many essential items of household expenditure are relatively insensitive to household size, eg housing and fuel costs. However, per capita incomes are a more useful guide to the purchasing power of the retired. Here, the 1971 Family Expenditure Survey implies a smaller disparity between the retired and the rest of the population, with a difference in average income per head of the order of 20% in 1971 (or about 42% in terms of income per adult).

3.3 There is considerable variation within this retired group, however, and a national average may be a poor guide to the small minority of retired people migrating to areas such as the South West.

3.4 Social Security statistics provide a strong pointer to the relative prosperity of the region's additional retireds and from these it is estimated that average household income in 1971 for the additional retireds in the South West was in the range of between £3 and £8 per week more than the national average for retired people.

3.5 It is unlikely that post-retirement employment is a significant contributory factor to these above-average incomes. Nationally, employment income in 1971 accounted on average for nearly 20% of the total incomes of one or two person households with heads aged 65 and over – the types of household likely to be most comparable with those of retired migrants. Employment income to households of the additional retired in the South West would be expected to be lower than this, if only because employment opportunities generally are in relatively short supply in the region's main retirement areas, particularly in the sort of office occupations for which most of the additional retireds are best suited.

3.6 What, then, are the sources of the relative income prosperity of the additional retireds in the South West? First, as noted elsewhere in the report, there is a very high incidence of home ownership among them. This incidence is directly related to their mobility, but is also likely to reflect above-average earnings in their working lives which could be expected to persist into retirement in the form of above-average incomes from occupational pensions or investments. There is indeed good reason to believe that both pensions and investments are significant factors. For example, estimates based on the Inland Revenue Personal Income Survey of 1969/70 point to an average income at that time from occupational and state pensions together of about £725 a year for the additional retireds' households in the South West compared with £515 for retired households generally. Estimates based on the same source suggest an average annual investment income among the additional retireds of nearly £400 a household, compared with some £75 a year for the typical non-migrant in the retired population.

3.7 In total, taking into account income from all sources, it is estimated that the average additional retireds' household in the South West was at the beginning of this decade receiving an annual income of around £1,500, compared with an average of £1,000 for all retirement households in the region and £900 for retirement households nationally. The income of all retirement households in the region would thus have accounted for about 14%, some £340 million, of the total personal income of the South West in 1971. The share of the additional retireds' in this would have been about £120 million. This represents about 5% of total personal incomes in the South West.

Expenditure of the retired

3.8 The expenditure of the additional retireds on goods and services produced within the region creates additional wealth for their local communities. This local component depends on the particular types of goods and services that retirement migrants buy, which may not be the same as for an average household. There is no direct information about the expenditure patterns of the retired in the region, but the data for retirement households on similar levels in the country as a whole provides a basis for estimates.

3.9 The estimates indicate that the additional retireds in the region spend more on housing and services than the average household nationally while expenditure on fuel, light and power is only slightly below average. Their expenditure on transport is considerably less than the national average (reflecting the lower level of car ownership among the retired) but more than the average for retired households nationally (reflecting income differentials). Like the retired generally, they spend comparatively little on food, although the difference as compared with younger households is probably a consequence of household size. For a given income level and household size, they also save relatively more than younger age groups.

3.10 The distribution of their personal expenditure between regional and extra-regional goods and services is probably such that the expenditure of a typical additional retireds' household would in 1971 have added some £450 per annum to local income, of which £285 would be employment income and the balance gross profits and other trading income (part of which might have accrued to residents of other regions). Applied to the estimates of the numbers of the additional retireds in the South West, this local income would amount to about £37 million for the region as a whole. For the Southern and Western sub-divisions alone, the figure would be about £27 million. Almost 90% of this income generation occurs within the service industries.

3.11 The capacity of the additional retireds for generating regional income implied by the estimates in the previous paragraph can be compared with an estimated figure of £115 million annually for the current (as opposed to capital) income-generating capacity of the South West's holiday industry (£75 million in the Southern and Western sub-divisions). The conclusion to be drawn is that, in terms of income for the local economies, the additional retireds are about a third as important as the holiday industry. But this is a conclusion that must be treated with caution, since it is suspected that the estimating basis on which the comparison is made understates the contribution of retirement. Also, unlike the holiday industry, retirement is not a seasonal phenomenon; employment generated by the presence of the additional retireds is more likely to be, if not full time, at least on a year round basis.

Local authority and hospital services

3.12 The assessment of the economic impact of retirement migration must also take into account the regional costs and benefits arising from demands on public services. These demands are chiefly in the health and welfare field, to which this part of the report is confined.

3.13 The previous section has estimated the increased regional income created by the personal expenditure of the additional retireds. To this must be added the extra income benefit generated by the extra activity in local authority and hospital services in the retirement areas in consequence of their presence. The likely scale of expenditure on these services is indicated by national estimates of the average level of social service benefits in kind to households headed by a retired person.

3.14 On the basis of these national estimates, it seems that expenditure on these public services by or on behalf of the region's additional retireds would have amounted to about £10 million in 1971. The bulk of the expenditure would accrue to local service activities with relatively little 'leakage' out of the region through purchase of pharmaceutical or other goods. In total, the estimated addition to regional income from this source would be of the order of £8 million a year, nearly all employment income. The employment generated in the health and welfare sectors is likely to have been particularly valuable in the major retirement areas of typically limited employment opportunity by providing jobs, and career prospects, for young people who might otherwise have had to move away.

3.15 The other side of the coin — the financial and other public costs imposed by the presence of the additional retireds — is not easy to assess quantitatively. But it is probably worth examining some of the concerns which are being expressed about this aspect, related particularly to the demands of retired people for health and welfare services. These concerns are not confined to, nor have they always originated in, the South West. Two main strands of argument can be identified. First, it may be argued that concentrations of elderly people create local pressures on real resources which lead to a lowering of the general standard of care and swamp any benefits arising from increased medical specialisation for the elderly. Second, even if there is no such effect on the overall efficiency or effectiveness of local health and welfare services, concentrations of old people may impose inequitable financial burdens on the community. But it may be simply that concentrations of old people make existing inadequacies in the services or inequalities in their mode of finance more publicly visible, especially since the additional retireds are likely to include a particularly articulate section of the elderly population.

3.16 This report, which is principally concerned with assessing the regional economic significance of retirement migration, cannot attempt to discriminate between these arguments in their relevance to the South West. In terms of a number of crude indicators such as the per capita provision of geriatric or welfare beds, the retirement areas of the South West appear to emerge as more favourably placed than, for example, similar areas in the South East region. But such statistics may not be a reliable guide to the quality of service available in retirement areas and one would need to examine the comparative requirements of migrants and non-migrants and the extent to which private residential accommodation was available to complement the public health and welfare provision. Furthermore, any deficiencies in that public provision cannot be attributed simply to concentrations of retired people but must also reflect inadequate planning for population growth or administrative rigidities in the capital budgeting procedures.

3.17 Real problems could arise with concentrations of elderly people in the region's retirement areas if it were not possible within the present organisation of the services to provide matching concentrations of staff in the required occupations or the necessary level of public funds for health and welfare facilities.

3.18 In practice, there does not appear to be any general problem in finding adequate professional staff to work in these very attractive areas, while the shortage of employment opportunities in much of the south and west of the region is conducive to the recruitment of clerical and manual workers from the local population. Where problems could arise in the future, and have been reported in some areas, is in finding people for personal service jobs, such as home helps, which are attractive to only a small minority of the local labour force but which do not offer the pay or status to attract people from other areas. The numbers involved are relatively small, however, and are not a fundamental test of the desirability or otherwise of future retirement migration.

3.19 The cost of public provision for the elderly and the means of financing it involve questions of public expenditure allocations and the relationship between central and local government finance which are quite outside the scope of this study. However, it may be noted that the effect of the rate support grant system is that retirement migration will on balance be 'profitable' in revenue terms – in the sense of relieving the rate burden – for local authorities which qualify for the resources element of the rate support grant. The majority of authorities in the retirement areas of the South West, with the notable exception under the former local government system of Torbay County Borough, qualify for these payments. For other authorities, retirement migration will be 'profitable' only so long as average per capita rate payments of the migrants are not too far below those of the resident population. The estimates of expenditure on housing by the region's additional retireds suggest that their average domestic rate payments would tend to be significantly higher than those of the population at large, though it is uncertain whether this would be the case in retirement resorts with particularly high rateable values.

Employment effects

3.20 The analysis earlier in this chapter of the patterns of expenditure by and on behalf of the region's retirement community makes it clear that the additional long-term employment generated by retirement migration into the region is likely to arise chiefly in the service industries' sector. Estimates suggest that, in a typical sub-region, the extra employment in service industries associated with each additional retired person would be of the order of 0·28 jobs. For most services, apart from retail distribution and local government, the proportionate effect of the retired seems significantly higher in this respect than that for the population as a whole. In one important case, medical and dental services, the ratio between employment and additional retirement is almost 60% higher than a comparable ratio for the working age population, However, if medical services are taken together with education, the other main age-dependent service, the employment ratios associated with the child and retired populations appear very similar and a little below the average for the working age group.

3.21 Applying these estimated employment-generating ratios to the additional retireds in the South West yields an estimate of 39,000 jobs as the local service employment dependent on the presence of the additional retireds – perhaps a total of 41,000 when allowance is made for the agriculture and manufacturing sectors. Of this, about three-quarters would be in Devon and Cornwall, broadly the Western and Southern sub-divisions, representing about 6% of the total employment in these areas. This compares with estimates that have been made elsewhere that about 12% of employment in the two counties is attributable to the holiday industry.

Investment

3.22 The regional 'turnover' attributable to retirement migration will include significant expenditure on capital account as well as current expenditure for the consumption demand of the additional retireds. Apart from a small amount of replacement investment, capital formation is primarily required to meet the needs of the increase in the region's retired population. The bulk of this investment will be in building construction, with a relatively low content of 'imports' from other parts of the country and could thus generate substantial local economic activity.

3.23 Various methods of estimating the capital requirements of the additional retireds in the South West point to an investment of about £2,400 (at 1968 prices) for each additional retired person, with the investment dividing roughly between the main sectors as follows:

Health and welfare services	12%
Other social capital	14%
Housing	51%
Other industrial capital	23%

Probably as much as 80% of this capital formation would be in the form of new buildings which would have to be provided by the region's construction industry. On this basis, the additional construction demand generated by the region's retirement migration would have amounted to about £9 million a year between 1966 and 1971, representing an additional employment in the region of about 3,100 jobs.

3.24 The housing element in the estimates above relates almost entirely to the private sector. Analysis of local variations in construction suggest that growth in the regional retirement migrants' population has had no effect on the rate of house-building in the public sector, but that one additional completion in the private sector has been associated with an increase of 3·13 persons in the numbers of the additional retireds. This ratio is noticeably larger than the estimates of the typical size of household among the additional retireds, implying that the housing stock in any area responds less than proportionately to numeric increases in housing requirements, at given levels of income etc. If this inference is right, it would follow that increased migration to an area would tend to raise house prices, encouraging both an increase in the average size of households and the conversion of more dwellings to multi-occupancy. Some increase in such conversions could be expected in any event to meet the needs of the older single-person households, eg widows, within the retired population.

3.25 Generalising from the estimates in the previous paragraph, the growth in retirement migration in the region between 1961 and 1971 might have increased the private housebuilding rate by some 1,000 dwellings a year, rising to perhaps as much as 1,500 in the second half of the decade. Assuming an average construction cost of £3,000 per dwelling, the equivalent rate of capital formation would have been about £4½ million a year in the latter period. Retirement migration would thus have accounted for 5% of new housing demand in the region, or 12½% in the Southern and Western sub-divisions alone.

3.26 Adding these capital estimates to those in paragraph 3.10 for current expenditure suggests that retirement migration provided employment for some 44,000 people in 1971 and added about £54 million to the income of the region. Virtually all of this additional activity would have been in the south and west of the region.

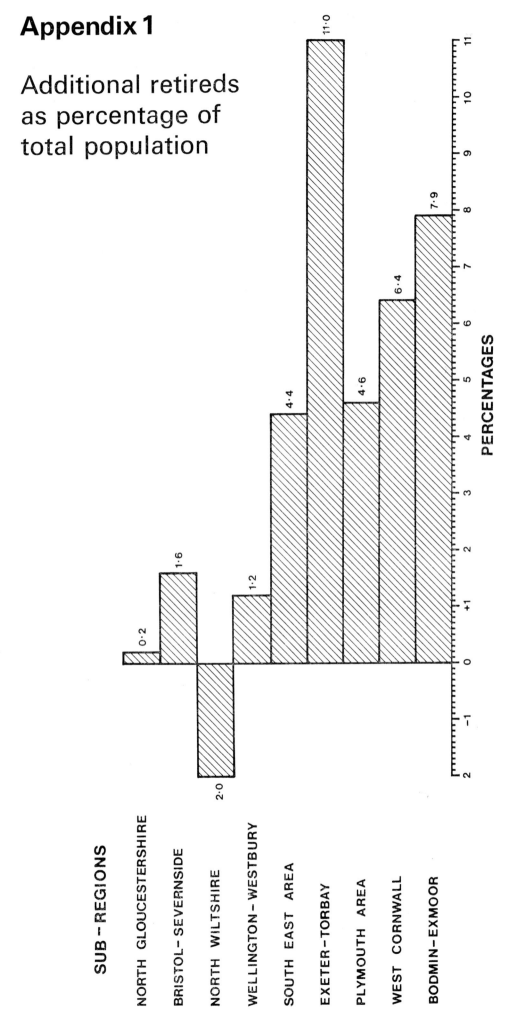

Appendix 1

Additional retireds
as percentage of
total population

SUB-REGIONS

NORTH GLOUCESTERSHIRE

BRISTOL-SEVERNSIDE

NORTH WILTSHIRE

WELLINGTON-WESTBURY

SOUTH EAST AREA

EXETER-TORBAY

PLYMOUTH AREA

WEST CORNWALL

BODMIN-EXMOOR

PERCENTAGES

0·2
1·6
2·0
1·2
4·4
11·0
4·6
6·4
7·9

Appendix 2

Trends in the population over retirement age, 1961-71, by economic planning area

Economic planning areas	Proportion of population over retirement age, 1961 (%)	Increase in population over retirement age, 1961-71				Estimated increase in 'additional retireds', 1961-71
		Numbers	Percentage increase	As percentage of total population, 1961	Percentage of population change, 1961-71	
1 Forest of Dean	13·8	1,900	27·0	3·73	80·8	300
2 Cotswolds	16·1	1,900	21·4	3.44	118·6	100
3 Severn Vale	14·8	10,000	21·6	3·20	27·0	−100
4 Bristol–Severnside	16·1	22,400	16·6	2·66	27·5	−4,700
5 Swindon	13·7	5,000	21·3	2·92	15·7	−600
6 West Wiltshire	13·0	4,500	26·1	3·39	29·3	200
7 Central Somerset– South West Wiltshire	17·0	3,500	21·7	3·68	22·5	400
8 Taunton– Bridgwater	16·7	5,600	25·5	4·26	32·4	1,400
9 Salisbury	14·7	2,200	18·3	2·69	23·8	−400
10 South Somerset– North West Dorset	17·0	4,900	24·9	4·23	40·9	1,200
11 North Dorset– South West Wiltshire	18·7	2,300	26·2	4·89	37·2	800
12 South West Dorset	18·1	5,000	25·5	4·61	90·3	1,100
13 South East Dorset	19·6	10,300	33·9	6·62	30·5	5,300
14 Exeter-East Devon	20·5	13,500	26·3	5·39	48·3	7,700
15 South East Devon	24·4	12,000	28·8	7·04	57·7	8,100
16 Plymouth	16·4	9,400	17·4	2·84	47·9	1,800
17 Exmoor	22·5	1,300	20·6	4·64	121·9	700
18 North Devon	20·2	4,800	25·0	5·04	42·6	2,600
19 North Cornwall– West Devon	19·8	2,600	17·1	3·40	93·0	800
20 West Cornwall	18·7	11,900	26·5	4·96	40·8	6,400
South West Region	17·1	135,000	22·5	3·84	35·4	33,000
Great Britain	14·7	1,199,000	15·9	2·34	38·4	—

Source: 1961 Census and 1971 Census advance analyses.

Appendix 3

South West Economic Planning Region[1]: sub-divisions, sub-regions and economic planning areas[2]

Sub-divisions	Sub-regions	Economic planning areas	Equivalent local authority areas
Northern	North Gloucestershire	1 Forest of Dean	County: Gloucestershire District: Forest of Dean (part)
		2 Cotswolds	County: Gloucestershire District: Cotswold (part)
		3 Severn Vale	County: Gloucestershire Districts: Cheltenham, Cotswold (part), Forest of Dean (part), Gloucester, Stroud (part), Tewkesbury
	Bristol-Severnside	4 Bristol-Severnside	Counties: Avon, Gloucestershire, Somerset Districts: Bath, Bristol, Kingswood, Mendip (part), Northavon, Sedgemoor (part), Stroud (part), Wansdyke, Woodspring
	North Wiltshire	5 Swindon	County: Wiltshire Districts: Kennet (part), North Wiltshire (part), Thamesdown
		6 West Wiltshire	County: Wiltshire Districts: Kennet (part), North Wiltshire (part), West Wiltshire (part)
Central	Wellington-Westbury	7 Central Somerset-South West Wiltshire	Counties: Somerset, Wiltshire Districts: Mendip (part), West Wiltshire (part)
		8 Taunton-Bridgwater	County: Somerset Districts: Sedgemoor (part), Taunton Deane
	South East	9 Salisbury	County: Wiltshire District: Salisbury (part)
		10 South Somerset-North West Dorset	Counties: Dorset, Somerset Districts: West Dorset (part), Yeovil
		11 North Dorset-South West Wiltshire	Counties: Dorset, Wiltshire Districts: North Dorset, Salisbury (part)
		12 South West Dorset	County: Dorset Districts: West Dorset (part), Weymouth and Portland
		13 South East Dorset	County: Dorset Districts: Poole, Purbeck, Wimborne (part)

continued

Sub-divisions	Sub-regions	Economic planning areas	Equivalent local authority areas
Southern	Exeter-Torbay	14 Exeter-East Devon	County: Devon Districts: East Devon, Exeter, Teignbridge (part), Tiverton
		15 South East Devon	County: Devon Districts: South Hams (part), Teignmouth (part), Torbay
	Plymouth Area	16 Plymouth	Counties: Devon, Cornwall Districts: Caradon, Plymouth, South Hams (part), West Devon (part)
Western	Bodmin-Exmoor	17 Exmoor	County: Somerset District: West Somerset
		18 North Devon	County: Devon Districts: North Devon, Torridge (part)
		19 North Cornwall-West Devon	Counties: Cornwall, Devon Districts: North Cornwall, Torridge (part), West Devon (part)
	West Cornwall	20 West Cornwall	County: Cornwall Districts: Carrick, Kerrier, Restormel, Penwith

1. Excludes Bournemouth and Christchurch Districts.

2. The South West Economic Planning Council have divided the region, for study purposes only, into 4 sub-divisions, 9 sub-regions and 20 economic planning areas. Map B in the Council's report, *A Strategic Settlement Pattern for the South West* (HMSO, 1974) illustrates the boundaries of the economic planning areas in relation to local government administrative areas.

Printed in England for Her Majesty's Stationery Office by J. Looker Ltd, 82 High Street, Poole, Dorset

Dd 289343 K16 8/75